Underwater Basket Weaving

A Continuing Education Course Guide

Fall Semester

Copyright © 2015 Lee Barret
All rights reserved.
ISBN: 978-1507828786
ISBN-13: 1507828780

Introduction

Underwater Basket Weaving is a slightly skewed take on adult Continuing Education Course Guides and offers a unique and compelling collection of credit courses, certificate courses, non-degree career training, workforce training, formal personal enrichment courses, self-directed learning, informal lab classes. experiential learning, problem solving and creative arts courses. Each course description is written by the course instructor. Classes are held in your community, at local schools, churches, gymnasiums and town halls.

Your future is in your hands, we hope you'll join us this semester!

Taco Nights: 1914 to Present

The Taco dates back to B.C. times, but the first documented Taco Feast was witnessed by Bernal Diaz del Castillo in the 1500's. As presented in Taco Nights 101: Origins (No longer avail.), it has been made clear that 'Taco Feasts' or 'Taco Nights' have been around as long as the taco itself. This course will focus on Taco Nights in modern times, covering the last 100 years only. We will look at how a changing world including industrialization, pesticide use, and the modernization of farming and technology have affected traditional Taco Nights. The evolution of language surrounding the Taco Night, such as the contemporary slang 'Taco Tuesday' and the history concerning the major toppings (cheese, tomato, lettuce) will also be covered.

Introduction to Mall Fudge Studies

From stores offering scented candles, far east imports, baggy khakis, lava lamps and ironic t-shirts, the mall of the 1970's & 80's replaced main street as the center for commerce in much of America. First introduced in the late 1800's, Fudge has been featured in Malls since their beginnings. In-fact many malls are permeated with the odor of their respective Fudgerys. This class will cover the basics of the exclusive history of Fudge sales, marketing & manufacturing in Malls. Including Fudge Sampling basics, Mall Fudge flavors, Mall Fudge origins, & dealing with Mall Fudge sales associates.

Business Wingdings

Wingdings is a font that renders alphabetic letters as mostly nonsensical symbols instead, such as a thumbs up, a triangle or a skull. Business Wingdings will teach you how to use this mostly useless,ignored and largely hated font in a Business setting, enabling you to jazz up your presentation or meeting. NOTE: If you intend to use wingdings in your place of work, it is highly suggested that all your co-workers also enroll in this class.

American Hidey Holes

Saddam Husseins 'spider hole', Anne Franks secret annex, Gerard Depardieu's career, history has shown us great hidey holes across the globe, but what about Americas Hidey Holes? In this course we will uncover the most important hidey holes of our own great nation. Starting with the basics like Ted Kaczynski and Henry David Thoreau's cabins, and moving into exclusive and less known hiding spots like Michael Jackson's 'peter pan room' and 'our secret special place' tool shed behind my Uncle Johns house. Prerequisite: Hiding in Plain Sight.

Finding Your Penis

This is a lab course that will help men or confused women locate their physical penis. This is not about finding your metaphorical penis or anything, this is about taking your pants off, identifying the crotch region and then locating your bacon rod. Instructor will help with the finding of your clam digger and light touching *will* occur. Instructor does not carry a MD but does have excellent thingy locating skills and prior meat bat findings under his belt. Instructor also has a giggle stick of his own but cannot guarantee he will find your kickstand especially if you are a woman or were born without a Mushroom-tipped love dart of your own. He will try though.

Finding Your Inner Penis (Finding Your Penis pre-req.)

Now that we've found your physical penis, its time to find your Inner penis. This course will teach you how to man up and act like you're working with a nice piece of pipe. Even if in 'Finding Your Penis' you found you had a small one,or none at all, this course will run through the basics of acting like a boss with a huge cock. Feel the confidence of what its like to have a big old weiner. Once you find your Inner Penis you'll get tables at crowded restaurants, be the life of the party and have people eating out of your hands. (for men or women)

Finding Your Outer Penis

This class will teach you how to act like a dick. There is a difference between inner confidence and pompous cockiness, but that being said, sometimes life calls for assertive arrogance, such as life threatening situations, business transactions, relationship problems or family dinners. This course will enable you to switch on your outer penis when the time comes.

Finding My Penis

Have you seen my Penis?

Shy Civil War Generals

Custer, Grant, Lee, these civil war generals are known for their big, bold and confident personalities. But history often overlooks the men that truly decided the outcome of the war, the timid, the apprehensive, the bashful leaders of the great conflicts who had immeasurable impact in losing & retreating and really made the great generals 'great' by way of their own weakness. This course will take an in-depth look at some of the most chagrined & sheepish leaders of the war including those who were reduced in-rank, Dishonorably Discharged, exiled or murdered by their own troops for their cowardly failures and flustered behavior. General Sam 'Shy Guy' Smith, General 'Weeping Willy' Bill Petcher, General 'Crying' Carl Jakes, General 'Pussy Pete' Hadden and other infamous & insignificant men of weak constitution are explored in depth in this course.

My Jellybeans

Color, size, flavor, shape, density, year of manufacture; there are endless methodologies to organization, categorization and correlation of your jellybean collection and if you're anything like me, you'll appreciate unlimited access to another collectors carefully curated archives. It should be noted that this course is about MY jellybeans and you will not be asked to bring in your own personal jellybean collection or any jellybeans at anytime. I will bring in my collection and you may look but not touch. No Buttered Popcorn jellybeans to be featured , I am a *Jellybean Puris*t and I have a complete collection without needing them.

Outros

First Impressions may define you, and are of course, based on your first introduction. But what about the last part of your first impression? The Outro? This class will focus on perfecting the outro in social and cultural situations. Make sure the last little part of your introduction is flawless. Exiting methods to be covered include 'The Irish Leave', 'The French Leave', 'The Black Leave', and many more.

Rap Album Skits 1994-1998

Pioneered in the late 1980's, humorous comedy skits helped define a certain period of hip-hop history. Used as album filler, segues between songs and interludes, the rap album skit usually consisted of common themes such as a telephone call, a voice mail, getting high, getting drunk, getting sex, getting guns, or talking shit about another rap artist with your friends in a threatening manner. Almost 75% of rap album skits ended with the sound of gunfire. One of the oddest innovations and annoying traditions of hip-hop and once standard on almost all rap albums, the rap album skit has now been nearly entirely phased out. We will look exclusively at the mid 1990's. the heyday of the rap album skit including sketches by Wyclef Jean, Biggie, Big Pun, Dr. Dre and the Wu Tang Clan.

Jellybeans for Puppies

Jellybeans are not meant for animals, but occasionally dogs will eat them. It is undeniable that puppies look cute eating jellybeans. This course will teach you proper puppy to jellybean pairings based on dog color/breed and jellybean color/flavor. Breed to flavor matching is very important. Advanced lessons will include teachings on how to change the color of your dogs feces based on jelly bean consumption. It is not advised that puppies eat more than 6 jellybeans a day. Puppies will be provided but PLEASE bring your own jellybeans.

Dog Dusting

To some 'dog dusting' is picking up their dog and dusting their homes with him as if he was a broom. To others its the act of lightly sprinkling anti flea powder on a dog. But in this course 'dog dusting' is the refined study of using a feather duster to lightly dust off your canine compadre. Before brushes or combs, before vacuums or pet groomers, ancient people would clean off their dogs with a light dusting. This class will examine the historical & cultural origins of dog dusting as well as teach students proper dog dusting procedure.

Bug Nuts
The katydid has testicles that make up 14% of its body weight (the equivalent of a 21 pound nuts on a 150 pound man), Carabid Beetles have only 1 testicle, fruit flies also have huge balls compared to body size. This course will examine these and other insect testicular compositions. While other insect anatomy will not be covered, students will leave this course with compressive understanding of the testicles of over 1,000 different bug species.

Why Do I Have Shingles?
In this course we will not examine the scientific or medical reasons for your shingles diagnosis but rather it will look at your general negative mental state and your ability to attract illness and bad luck because of your crappy outlook on life and your cynical attitude. This class will cover the bad choices and wrong decisions surrounding the 6 months around your shingles illness.

This Only Happens to Other Families
Right?

Marley & Me
This exciting music appreciation and culture course will teach you about my relationship with Bob Marley, the reggae singer. I first heard Bob Marley when playing hacky sack in the quad of my college many years ago, since then, through extensive listening of the album 'Legend", drug use, heavy drum circle participation and fragmented reading of rasta religious texts, I have become an expert of sorts. This dynamic course will take you from that first listen, into my light marijuana experimentation right through my dreadlock phase. I'll try and remember as much as I can, classes will be held in your dorm room. (The course instructor would like to note that this course and its title have been offered since 1992 and predate any films or novels sharing the same title.)

Business Tights
For both men and women, Business Tights will take an engaging look at womens fashion in the business environment. Gone are the days of power suits, shoulder pads and pants suits, but tights are back. Thicker than pantyhose and sheerer then leggings, tights walk the fine line between sexy and classy, allowing slight hints of sexual power and influence in the workplace.

Advanced Business Tights
With the fundamentals learned in 'Business Tights', this advanced program will cover such subjects as printed and colored tights, the fetishisation of tights in the workplace, and interdisciplinary tight usage, such as using athletic or renaissance-era tights for business.

Describing Movie Parkour To Your Mother

A course designed for anyone having difficulties verbally imparting the kinetic beauty of a Luc Besson movie to their mothers. Our instructor will lead you away from using the degrading words found in a gymnasium to describe movie Parkour and enable our students to find more appropriate ways to tell their moms about "this scene in this movie that my buddy Steve showed me where this guy hops a fence, tic-tacs up a fire escape then, out-of-nowhere cat-leaps his crotch to some Korean gangsters face who's been holding his girl hostage the whole time." to their mothers. The course consists of an hour long seminar on technique building and creative describing, followed by an hour long workshop of one-on one parkour describing to guest Moms and Grandmothers (all guest speakers will initially have no idea what Parkour is and little idea of what anyone in the class is even talking about).

Diagnosing Horse Nightmares

Elephants might never forget, but horses have big dreams. Highly sociable and extremely on edge, horses require a high level of attention in order to maintain good health. It is common knowledge that horses suffer terrible nightmares that affect their mental well being. This in depth course will give you the expertise needed to properly diagnose horse nightmares. Through hoof reading, ear motion sensitivity training, manure study and staring into the horses eyes we will be able to find the source of these bad dreams, and free the animal from its terrifying grip. *(Please bring your own horse)*

Space Dragon Drawing

Hey guys, lets get together and draw wicked space dragons! Whether its your first space dragon or your one millionth galaxy flying fire breathing beast, everyone is welcome here! We will start with the basics, drawing space dragons on the covers of 3-ring binders of other courses and then move into sharpie on denim, rockin' full size jean jacket dragons! Extra credit for creating a cool name for our crew, we can all wear the jackets around town! Advanced studies will move into sick space dragon airbrush work and the course will culminate in everyone painting a wicked space dragon mural on my van!

Real Estate for Outer Space

The next logical place to develop and build condominiums and mini malls will be space. If you are as convinced of this as I am, this is the course for you. I don't know much about the science and engineering required to actually build in space, but I do have my Real Estate license and I'll cover marketing ideas, how to be a 'people person' and build rapport and how to pre-qualify prospects and introduce them to your preferred lender. We will also discuss putting those habitat bubbles on the moon and decide what the price per square foot seems fair for the planets in our immediate solar system.

Introduction to Pretending to know the Constellations
Tired of being shown up by at cocktail parties and barbeques by home Astronomers and back-yard stargazers touting their celestial knowledge and comprehensive expertise of the constellations? This class will give you the fundamentals for faking your way through pointing skyward and naming the timeless shapes in the stars. While actual constellations will not be covered, this course will arm you with an arsenal of real sounding constellation names and abstract shape finding, defining, and pointing skills.

Daytime Firefly Hunting
Anyone can catch fireflies at night. This class isn't for anyone. Armed with a butterfly net and a whiffle bat, students will be graded on their ability to do the impossible – catch fireflies during the day. Never mind that, even if fireflies *weren't* nocturnal, they'd be invisible in daylight. Good luck, fuckers.

Speed Calligraphy: the Art of Lettering with Disappearing Ink
Calligraphy is a timeless art form. What this class presupposes is... maybe it isn't? Designed for masters of the calligraphic arts, this intense lab teaches students to cope with imperfection for the sake of speed... for its own sake. Pen and parchment will be provided but disappearing ink is the responsibility of the student. Stock up at any magic store or gag depot. Please note: this class guarantees you get carpal tunnel.

Hiking at Home
In this age of Twitter and online shopping, the only reason to leave home is to get some exercise and experience the great outdoors. Not anymore. This 4-credit course teaches students how to re-imagine their homes as bonafide hiking trails. The first 12-and-a-half weeks will be devoted to safety, then students will execute challenging hiking routes in their very own homes. Using rustic potpourri and scented candles, students will learn to trick the senses into thinking they've actually ventured into the wild. Strategically placed stuffed animals can also enhance the experience. Learn how to hike from the living room to the bedroom; from the bedroom to the living room, and as a final project – from the living room to the bedroom and back.

The Philosophy of Plantlife And Death
The question we all struggle with, 'what is the meaning of plantlife and death?' will be discussed in this emotional and engaging course. Is plant here to serve man? Is man here to serve plant? Is plant here to serve plant? We will struggle with these questions and more, just as I have. And after it's life, what is the meaning of plant death?

Sand Castle Demolition
Destroying a child's imagination and turning your oppressive actions into their repressive behavior takes tact and skill. Sand Castle Demolition explores the relationship between creativity, expression and the symbolic killing of a child's hopes and dreams. *Offered in the Summer only.

Texting While Driving (intro)

Speed Limits, stop signs, red lights, police, mothers pushing strollers, korean lady drivers, it's hard enough to drive as it is, without the added need of using your thumbs to type unimportant messages to friends and family. When they started putting radios in cars they said the same thing, that it was a dangerous distraction, but we adapted! Texting While Driving will give you the essential skills needed for the modern multitasking driver, skills for when you absolutely must notify someone you are 'almost there'. The one hand text and the more difficult two hand text will be covered first, then we will move into rapid eye movement from phone to road and back again. We will also learn how to safely drop the phone into your lap upon seeing a police car.

Introduction to Texting During a Real Life Conversation

"Man do I really need to listen to this guy talk though this whole meal?" Don't be ashamed, it's a common thought these days. There are so many other places you could be right now, why not at least check in and see what you're missing? In this course, we will look at a few methods of texting while you are also supposed to be engaged in a real human interaction. From the polite methods of accompanying your texting with a verbal apology to the more crass method of simply focusing on your phone through an entire conversation, we will cover it all. We will also look at this interaction from the other side, and work on verbal and physical cues to win back the attention of a texter in a social interaction. Like smashing her phone on the floor, the bitch.

Clandestine Texting

Cheating on the husband, setting up dates under the family dinner table or coyly texting an ex are all very real parts of our modern social world. In Clandestine Texting we will learn the skills needed to successfully text when you're not suppose to, or who you're not suppose to. Basic techniques like texting under the boardroom meeting table, texting in the bathroom with the shower running and texting from 'your' side of the bed will be discussed as well as more advanced texting methods like entering phone numbers under a fake name for men or women you shouldn't be texting, archiving and storing/deleting of inappropriate texts and more. We will also learn skills to maintain an emotionless facial expression when receiving a steamy text, enabling you to receive any text anywhere! Case studies will include Tiger Woods.

Sexting for Teens

Moms on your case, Dads got his nose in your business, you got no space of your own, except your phone? In Sexting for Teens we will study this new method of courting from top to bottom. Over the course of the semester you will text directly with your instructor (me). Starting with light flirting and soon moving into more advanced and disarming sexual language like 'pic 4 pic', 'send dik pik' and 'let me see dat ass' you will learn the skill of sexting from a first hand perspective. This course is not held in a classroom, simply enroll by texting me your age/sex/location as soon as you'd like to begin at 212-938-1290. After several weeks of increasing texting, when I text you about meeting me at the Galleria it means I am ready to give you your Completion of Course Keepsake. Must be over 13 but under 18 to enroll.

Intro to Feigning Environmental Sustainability
Lets face it, these days If you're not into bringing your own grocery bag to the store, recycling, fuel economy, organic food, saving the whales and cleaning the oceans then you're a nobody. But keeping up on all of that is time consuming and expensive. In this course we will give you the basic skills needed to at least APPEAR like a Whole Foods shopping enviro warrior. We will give you the talking points to fool anyone!

Short Story in 140 Characters or Less
In our modern landscape many writers have to convey an entire story in less than 140 characters. This course will teach methods on writing w

Perspective
I think its time you got a little perspective on things. Don't you? One by one students will be asked to lay their life story out in front of the class, and then as a group, using our own life experiences as reference points, we will put your shit into perspective.

How to Forget Your Password
These days everything requires a password, online banking, email accounts, sex fetish discussion forums; this course is for those of you who are neatly organized, and have your passwords written down all in one place, or have them all memorized. Through extensive course work, we will teach you how to use multiple passwords that are easily forgettable, write these passwords on tiny easy to lose scraps of paper, and even teach you how not to write down passwords at all. By the end of this class you'll be clicking 'reset password' links for every website you visit just like everyone else!

Cultivating a Bookshelf to Impress
Who has time to read these days? With endless cat videos on youtube, 3 televised singing competition shows and hacked nude teen disney star phone pictures to look at, curling up with a good book is next to impossible. But that doesn't mean you can't *look* well-read. This course will teach you how to cultivate a bookshelf meant to impress even the casual dinner guest, without having to read anything! Choosing impressive book spines is an art form in itself. We will cover the basics of building a book collection that says any of the following: 'spiritual', 'well rounded', 'well traveled', 'cultured', 'snooty', 'snotty', 'witty', 'black friendly', 'feminist', and 'yuppie asshole'.

Deconstructing Harry
In this 3 day lab class, my friend Harry will come into the room and we will deconstruct him. On the first day we will deconstruct his clothing and outward appearance. On the 2nd day we will pry into his emotional psyche. On the 3rd day we will pull Harry apart limb by limb. (Harry is ok with this).

Revenge Tagging in Social Media
Slighted at a party by someone who you thought was your friend? This course will help you develop the skills to seek revenge in the modern way; via social media. How to post and tag ugly and compromising photos of others, how to post embarrassing facts on peoples walls and more.

Their, There, and They're: A class for fucking idiots.
Typically around the age of, oh I don't know, 7, people have figured out when to use "their" "there" or "they're". This class is for all you fucking idiots who still don't get it. We'll also go over shit like "two" "too" and "to" because why the hell not? God knows none of this is getting through your thick skulls anyways.

Writing on Mushrooms.
In this 100 level course we explore the writing process, with a focus of writing on mushrooms.

Writing *On* Mushrooms.
In this 200 level course we explore the writing process, with a focus of writing on mushrooms.

Writing on *Mushrooms*.
In this 300 level course we explore the writing process, with a focus of writing on mushrooms.

Introduction to How the Sausage is Made
This class will focus on the big questions surrounding the pork production, odors, and sales of America's 2nd favorite breakfast meat. You can expect to dive "wrist deep" into the colorful world of brats, brocks, and hot Italians. This class will NOT cover Scrapple. Students who do not drop out after the first class will learn that there's a lot more to smashing churned meats and spices into an indigestible casing than they ever knew. *This class satisfies 1 Diversity Requirement.

Intro 2 Biz
Biz is what we in the biz call business. Intro is short for introduction. 2 is a cool way of writing "to". You're only reading the course description and you've already learned so much. Do yourself a favor and sign up for this class. You know you want to, I know you want to, so just stop beating around the bush and just do it. I mean, it doesn't even start until 2pm. 2pm! How great is that? If this is your first class of the day you're gonna get to sleep in until like noon if you want to. Ok, I'll see you there.

Child Making
It's a fucking class.

How to Litter
In today's modern society littering can be difficult. This class will begin with things like "accidentally" missing the trashcan, throwing cigarette butts out the window, and then move on to more advanced materials like styrofoam. Halfway through you will be expected to keep a littering journal to be turned in at the end of the semester, and then scattered around campus.

Pretending to listen to NPR
In this Introductory class we'll go over various "big" names that every person pretending to listen to NPR should know. You'll learn a broad cast of broadcasters from Terry Gross to Lakshmi Singh, as well as how to complain about pledge drives. Note: this class is based on Los Angeles NPR and Los Angeles NPR only. And I'm talking KPCC, not any of that KCRW, we play hipster music but also have NPR shows BS. This class is a prerequisite for Advanced NPR Pretending: Podcasts.

Advanced NPR Pretending: Podcasts
In Introduction to NPR Pretending, you learned how to speak over your friends at dinner parties, how to treat waiters with disdain while ordering cuisine that is not on the menu, and how to mention casually – yet constantly – that you do not own a television set. This course will expand upon that paradigm and guide students into the benefits of talking at length about Podcasts about personal finance, interior design, and quinoa that they did not enjoy listening to in the first place. This class may be taken as a Pass/Fail. However, all students are required to be unbearable.

BCC'ing for BBWs
As the 21st century approached, numerous innovations led to an exponential growth in technology. From the rice farmer in China to the banker on Wallstreet, this growth has touched everyone's lives. BCC'ing for BBWs (Blind Carbon Copying for Big Beautiful Women) will explore technology basics, in a relaxed and intimate environment. Curriculum includes: Moore's law, computer coding, and Ruben's "Venus at the Mirror."

Poor Now :(Rich Someday :) Crafting American Fortune Cookies in the 21st Century
Beginning in the 1970s, income inequality or the "Great Divergence," and Chinese Buffets, began to steadily increase. Today a lack of economic mobility has brought desperation and despondency to millions of hardworking Americans. This apathy has only been tempered by the wonderful and enduring Horatio Alger myth; anyone who works hard can make it from rags to riches. Chinese lenders, evaluating the American market, have reinforced this myth with the creation of the fortune cookie. This course seeks to understand the motivations behind the fortune cookie's creation and consumption

Vicious Bee Species
There are nearly 20,000 known bee species and over 10,000 unknown. Bees exist on every continent but Antarctica Of the 20,000 known species, several dozen are known to be outright Vicious. This course will take an in-depth look at just the vicious species. Bee provocation will be studied in a clear glass box at the front of the class, and each student will have a 5 minute chance to enter the box and witness the viciousness of the vicious species first hand. Lab fee: $15 per bee death. Bee's provided.

The Tweed Jacket in 20th Century Western Clothing Design
From the time of its origins in Scotland, the Tweed jacket has been associated with the upper classes and their elite leisure and recreation activities. Throughout the 1900's the tweed jacket in western societies has stylistically remained mostly unchanged but its meaning has been re-appropriated multiple times. The choice of early motorists, golfers and hunters and later of ivy league professors of the 1940's - 60's the tweed jacket was nearly forgotten in the mod 60's when Herringbone and Houndstooth surpassed it in popularity. Though never completely abandoned by the elderly or stuffy british men, Tweed survived and re-emerged in the 90's to be embraced by preppies, punks, professors and everyone in-between. Seen as an ironic choice for anti-establishment types, a classy option for pipe-smoking thirty something douchebags and as a sincere symbol of sophistication and heritage for others, this class will look at Tweed inside and out, leather elbow patches or not. (You must wear a Tweed jacket to class)

Potential History: What Could Have Happened
While history defines who we are as a people, Potential History takes an indepth look and what might have been. From global hypotheticals like 'What if Hitler Succeeded?', to 'What if Blacks were White?' to national suppositions like 'What if the South had Won the Civil War?' to 'What if Biff really DID change history with the Sports Almanac?' this course aims to cover a broad spectrum of 'what could have been'.

7 Baby Tips Parents Wont Tell You
This course will feature parenting advice and baby facts shared by men and women who have never, not for a day, been a parent. Students will be instructed by sterile or barren professors who have spent little to "zero" time around living babies. From the obvious "Ugh! Don't bring your baby to lunch." To the erudite "rubbing cinnamon on a baby's head will make it smarter." This class is must for prospective friends of people who will probably breed. *But probably should.

7 Baby Tips Babies Wont Tell You
If only babies could simply TELL us what they want, things would be so much easier!! Well now they have,well they didn't tell you, but they told me...and now I'm telling you! This is NEXT LEVEL SHIT.

Cruzin' : For Women

Cruzin' takes a certain combination of confidence, coolness, and coyness. Historically 'Cruzin' or 'Crusin' meant the action of looking for a sexual partner on the streets. In this context that definition can be applicable, but we will primarily be looking at cruzin in the contemporary sense, meaning to aimlessly drive a car for pleasure. This course will focus on the fundamentals for Cruzin in western environments and on both paved and dirt roads. This class is for women only and enrollment is limited to 4.

The History of History Channel

Debuted on January 1st, 1995, The History Channel quickly established itself as THE channel for well educated, stiff white men over the age of 31. Early on referred to as 'The Hitler Channel' for its extensive use of programming centered on World War II, the channel soon became known for offering detailed and historically accurate material packaged in entertaining ways. With 65% of viewers being home owners and 30% holding college degrees, The History Channel proves a great avenue for marketing to a intelligent and thoughtful viewer base. This course will begin with the genesis of the channel and culminate in recent times, when The History Channel removed the 'The' and "Channel' from its name, and just became known as 'History'.

How to Judge a Book By Its Cover

Aside from reading a book, the only other way to judge a book is by its cover. This class will teach students the proper approach to judging a book by viewing and analyzing its dust jacket, hardcover or paperback artwork, including font, image, artwork and overall design composition. Students will be able to draw conclusions on the subject and plot of books based purely on appearance with the skills acquired in this course.

Playing Dumb

Many times in a difficult or stressful situation it is advisable to play dumb to avoid further conflict or to get to a desired result. This course will elaborate on an ability most of us naturally excel at and refine your skills even further. Playing dumb is of course different than actually being dumb, and it is advisable that actual dumb students do not enroll. Situational hypotheticals and role playing will be used including basic playing dumb scenarios such as: 'hey who drank my last beer?', 'Who scratched mom's car?' to more complex situations like 'where are my panties?' and 'have you seen the baby?'.

Advanced Potato Peeling

While many home chefs and cooking mothers consider their kitchen skills second-to-none, this comprehensive potato peeling course aims to raise your culinary skills to a master level. Students will learn to peel using a variety of peelers including the: lancashire peeler, Y-peeler, Rex peeler, yoke peeler, speed peeler, French Peeler, Aussie Peeler as well as straight razor, pocket knife and hand peeling. Potato grip, finger placement, handle skills and peel motion will be covered. Eye removal will be practiced as well. Additional Lab Fees apply if students cannot bring their own Potatoes.

Animal Trickery

Many animals in the wild rely on trickery, deception, subterfuge or deceit to stay alive. This course does not deal with animal - to - animal trickery, but instead focuses on human - to - animal trickery. We will focus on learning a variety of skills best applied to fooling animals into bending to your will and manipulating their behavior. Practical jokes and animal pranks will also be covered.

Animal Husbandry (Marrying Animals)

Some schools offer a course called 'Animal Husbandry' which focuses on the breeding, domestication and raising of animals. This course takes that practice one step further. Many species of animals are known to pair off for life, some for one mating season. Like humans, animals should have the right to marry a partner of their own choosing. Animal Husbandry will teach you the basics of helping animals select their mates, as well as navigate the sometimes difficult stages of marriage.

Dildos & Dildonts 102: (The Ins & Outs of Dildo Ownership)

This course will guide you from A-Z on the requirements of owning a dildo. Purchasing online or in person, Gag Gifting, Fantasy / Role Playing use, Ironic party and other non-bedroom uses as well as public vs. private uses will be covered. Nervous joke making with sex shop cashout girl will be practiced in role-playing scenarios, Professor may also suggest other role-playing games on a case by case analysis. Understanding proper cleaning, maintenance and appropriate storage & hiding methods will also be covered. NOTE: Dildo Excuses, Double Headed Dildos and Strap On Dildos will be covered in: *Dildos & Dildont's 202: Dild-efintly-* offered in Spring only.

The Evolution of Creationism

Even Creationism wasn't born perfect and complete. This course will take a look at the evolution of creationism as a belief and theory. Starting with its description in the Jewish Torah and moving through its many changes through medieval Christianity, Protestant Reformation, James Ussher and its many interpretations across nations and cultures. We will look at its evolution across different cultures including Islam, Judaism, Hindu and Christian and cover the 12 main types of creationism including; young earth, gap, old earth, day age, progressive, neo, Intelligent Design, Creation Science, Theistic evolution, Flat-Earth and the Omphalos hypothesis

Indian Reservation Casino Management

This course will explore today's career opportunities for Native Americans, primarily focusing on the booming industry of Indian gaming. Experts and casual observers are calling casino management "the new buffalo." Want to know how to manage a casino on tax-exempt land? Whether you're a white man or a savage – this class will show you *how*.

Smelling Yard Sale Toys

Whether your interest is smelling yard sale toys with the intent of buying or smelling just for pleasure, this course will give you the fundamental tools needed for proper smell execution and enjoyment. The course will teach both clandestine and forthright sniffing techniques as well as lessons for refining your olfactory palate for known used-toy smells.

Important Michaels

Michael Jackson, Michael J. Fox, Michael Jordon, Michael Bolton, Michael Keaton, Michael McDonald, Michael Caine, Michael Landon, Michael Buffer, Michael Douglas, and dozens of other Michaels will be covered in this exciting class about Michaels. We won't be going into depth on each Michael, we will just list Michaels.
Prof. Michaels

Raising Flutie

Born October 23rd 1962 in Manchester Maryland, Doug Flutie is recognized as one of the great underdog stories in sports history. This course will focus not on his sporting accomplishments but on his parents Dick and Joan Flutie and their manner of raising Doug. Several major family events will be studied including his family move to Florida when he was 6, where his father, Richard, worked as an engineer in the aerospace industry. After the dramatic slow-down of the space program in the mid-1970s, the Flutie family again moved in 1976 to Natick, Mass. Flutie family holidays, birthdays and meals will also be covered.

Hey Man Wanna Get Some Wings?

For some men, the ability to ask this question comes naturally, to others it comes harder, and for some it is downright impossible. Designed for those men not so lucky to learn the real world skills needed to survive in man culture from a father figure, this course will take you through the fundamentals of the manly ritual of enjoying wings together at a bar or pub. The causal proposal, the firm suggestion and the alpha-male style assertion of wing getting will be covered. Wing invite declination will also be covered as well as aversion tactics like 'naa the old lady is waiting', to 'na bro, I gotta go tap this piece I met last night'. Dealing with condemnation of the man group with attacks you will encounter like 'come on ya fag!' to be looked at too. Various levels of spicy-ness to be covered and tasted during our field studies. Carrot Stick, Blue Cheese & Celery will not be covered

Making Your Way in the World Today

Making your way in the world today takes everything you've got. Taking a break from all your worries sure would help a lot. Wouldn't you like to get away?
Supplies required for class: Name-tag.

Come In, We're Doing a Puzzle

We'll start with the edge pieces first. 4 credits.

We Bloggin'
Dying to tell friends, strangers and people from high school what you ate, watched, read or heard today? We Bloggin' will take you through the A-Z's of sharing every mundane detail of your day through internet journaling. Photo sharing, witty one liners, proper use of 'best (blank) ever...', will be studied as well as casual and full on bragging tactics. Strategies for making your dinner, night out or vacation seem better than everyone else's will be covered.

Prepositions: How to dangle them
What if I told you that in 4 short months you could get 3 college credits without having to anything but show up for class and take a few notes? Not bad, eh? Now what if I sweetened the pot a little? What if I told you, and you can quote me on this, that taking this class would lead to some big things? Things that you, if I know you (and I think I do), might interest you? Cars? Money? Fame? Success? Is it going to be easy? Does a snake have a neck? Just sign up below and let's see if it all works out. 3 Credits. This is going to be great, trust me.

So You Want to Sell Dolphin Meat?
Using only slideshows and sound effects, world-renowned adventurer, butcher and author Fred Framp sheds a light on the pros and cons of entering the international dolphin meat market. Students will be required to sample several different cuts and cooking techniques throughout the semester. Questions will not be encouraged nor answered. *This class will have a "splash zone."

Cool Shirts
What makes one "Lizard Wearing Sunglasses" shirt a success while another "Lizard Wearing Sunglasses" shirt falls flat? When is a stain *more* than a stain? Where do those people with the body odor find the best vintage shirts? This 16-week course will answer these important questions and so many more. Employees of Urban Outfitters will not be allowed to take this class.

Introduction to Giant Check Holding
This course will focus on holding large novelty checks over your head with style and sophistication. Using techniques acquired from industry professionals in the fields of golf, game shows, and charitable donations, students will learn the "tricks of the trade." Each student will be required to hold an large check over their head for the first and last 15 minutes of each class and to act surprised and delighted when the professor points at them. Grading will be based on showmanship, emotional believability, and making sure the check is facing the correct direction (forward).

Treating Pizza Bagel Burns
You couldn't wait, could you? I know, I know, it was the first thing you ate today after skipping dinner last night to hang out with Melissa. The good news is that toaster oven you found under the stuffed animals in the children's book section works like a charm. Hey, I'm not blaming you for liking it a little burnt. The way the cheese gets that brown color and the entire bagel, not just the outsides, has that satisfying crunch. But, face it, Bucko, you could've at least blown on it a few times before diving right in.

Hernias
By the end of the semester, students will be able to correctly say the following while wincing with every breath: "Did I blackout and eat a screwdriver? I know what this is. Can you drive me to the hospital? Thanks, breh, I owe you one."

Unmixing Chex
This lighthearted class is a must for aspiring OCD sufferers and future meth addicts. Students will learn how to identify the 6 major ingredients in Chex Mix and Chex Mix: Bold, separate each element into an appropriate storing container, and how to dispose of the stale individual ingredients by feeding them to birds. *Required Materials include: 1 Bowl, 1 Forceps, 1 Pair of Safety Goggles, 1 Magnifying Glass, 2 Latex gloves, 1 2nd Bowl, 1 Lead Apron, 1 Bag of Chex Mix of Chex Mix Bold.*

Introduction to listening to people on cocaine
This online course will teach you're the 3 techniques of maintaining a conversation with someone who just snorted powder cocaine: 1) Laugh every 6 seconds no matter what happens 2) "Nah, man, Steve DIDN'T just give you a weird look. He's cool." 3) Making every other word a superlative. An inflated sense of confidence is required throughout this course.

Arranging Your Very First Gangbang
Opening your door to the world of group sex is a rewarding life-long adventure that begins when you sign up for this class. Licensed instructors will take you by the hand and gently teach you're the ins and outs of hosting or attending your first groupfuck. Topics will include but are not limited to: What should I wear? Who to start licking first? Showing your vagina to a guy you sometimes see at Safeway. Who's cookin' what? That goes there OR there. When 10 boxes of Baking Soda isn't enough and your wife is coming home in an hour. All ages and ethnicities welcome. 3 credits.

North Dakota: Mount Rushmore is that way
This course offers students a shortcut through the Roughrider State so that they'll be able to reach the only almost-interesting attraction in this God forsaken land. Students will be implored to avoid 99% of this barren dead-end that was stolen from the Indians and given to white people so boring that Josh Duhamel is their most famous export. Did we mention that North Dakota has the highest churches per capita of any state? Yeah, so go see those big ol' stone heads and then get the hell out of there. 1 Credit.

Restaurant Reservations 101 - How to reserve a table
www.opentable.com OMG You just gotta try the tempura rock shrimp appetizer. 3 credits.

Restaurant *Reservation* 101 - getting over your fear of waiters
Always pacing, always lurking close by, always watching. You're not alone with your paralyzing fear of waiters. In this course we will use real world situations to help you move past your crippling server anxiety. Lab Fee: I choose the restaurants, you cover the bill.

Working For The Weekend
This course will uncover the mysteries behind the lifecycle of hardworking grunts who bust their humps to put hot chew on the table. Topics covered will include: Having time to lean = Having time to clean, Being a "Yes Man" and liking it, saving up for that boat that will never happen, and learning to like paintball. Students who take this class might fall into a crippling depression, especially during the "Your Cubicle, Your Friend" section of the curriculum, when faced with the distinct possibility of a lifetime of meaningless work. Therapists will be available for post-class session on M/W/F. 3 Credits or 5 Credits if used at the company store.

Stepdad Raps
"This class is cool, so don't be a fool, I'm payin for your school, so don't you drool. Just take this class, and I'm sure you'll pass, or your mother and I will kick your ass." Too many Lectures. Not enough Discussion.

Moccasins and Water Moccasins: A History of Slippers and Snakes
Psst. Hey, Mr. What's that by your foot? Yeah, that brown thing. What the hell is that? Is it a snake or a comfortable style of footwear made out of deerskin and colored beads? Psst. What do you mean you're not sure? You'd better take this class, Mr.

Learn about the exciting shared history of slippers and snakes with a professor who has over 27 years of experience as a herpetologist and owner of "The Glast Slipper" shoe store- Prof. Lyndon Glast. 3 Credits. (Teacher's Assistant is a quarter-blood Winnebago Indian)

Life on the Edge: A Shaky Guide to Shaving Your Scrotum with a Straight Razor
FACT: All primates groom themselves and their partners. DOUBLE FACT: Shaving your pubic hair with a disposable razor is for poor people. For generations, men in the western hemisphere have been removing their pubic hair with straight blades for comfort, convenience, and the illusion of increased phallus size. In this course, FACT: We will teach you how to shave your scrotum. DOUBLE FACT: We will teach your how to shave your scrotum with a straight blade razor just like the kind your grandfather used to shave his face with. FACT: Students will be required to show before and after photographs of their genitals to receive class credit. DOUBLE FACT: It will look bigger. 3 credits.

Sock management

Brown socks. Black socks. White socks. Argyle socks. Socks with stripes. Funny socks. Stockings. Socks for animals. Holes. Where do they go and when do you where them? This course will not have a final. Any student who does not attend 100% of the discussions will fail this class. Overflowing top left dresser drawer required.

Lying to Your Self

This course will focus on the art and science of justifying anything in order to pass/project their blame/shortcomings onto others. Throughout the semester students will tell themselves that they are finally going to use the gym membership they've had for 2 years and get in the best shape of their lives, that there just aren't any good guys/girls in this town, and continue to convince themselves that they have artistic abilities that deserve attention and financial compensation. Only students with way above average IQs will be accepted.

Lying to Your Wife

This course will focus on the 2 major principles of dealing with an inquisitive wife: Deception & Distraction. Unmarried male and lesbian students will learn valuable lessons in hiding affairs, hiding alcohol around the house, hiding income, and hiding in the shed until she goes to her sister's house. Can one unsolicited compliment after years of neglect save a marriage? We like to think so.

Advanced Lumberjacking, Ebay class: Accelerating your Axe Seller Rating.

Nice picture, idiot. No one is ever going to buy that handmade Gränsfors Bruks with that pawltry description, dumbass. Jesus, have you ever even sold an axe online before? Doubt it. Here let me show you.

"The War of Northern Aggression" and other ridiculous things people from the south say.

Are y'all "fixin" to learn about the South? Well "bless your heart!" I mean, listen y'all, this here "might could" be the most important class y'all ever take. Find out why we call all soda "Coke." Why the term "alcoholic" doesn't apply is someone was "in the war." Are you "more fucked up than a soup sandwich?" Do people tell you that "you're like a blank piece of paper: Don't say nothing"? Are you currently "higher than a giraffe's pussy?" So "stupid you couldn't pour piss out of a boot if their were instructions on the heel"? Well, listen up, because here's what's up: This class isn't "as hard as Chinese 'rhtmitic." 3 hours.

Introduction to Not Having to Have Dad Touch Me There Sometimes

This is hands-on learning at it's finest. Participation is mandatory. Don't tell your mother. Seriously.

Radical Islamic Studies

This course is designed to give students the opportunity to discuss the controversial topic of Radical Islam and it's role in media and society. Through peaceful discussions students will peel back the layers of anger and hatred that cause division both domestically and abroad. Guest speakers and selected works by theologians will round out the curriculum and hopefully give curious students insight as to why these crazy motherfuckers keep blowing shit up.

Honors Geography Seminar: Memorizing State Birds

This Honors course will primarily focus on the 50 United States and the 50 birds that represent them. The Northern Flicker, the Lark Bunting, the Black-capped Chickadee… Finally, you'll have something to talk to your Grandmother about while playing UNO.

Comparative Literature 712: Comparing the Thickness of Some Boring English Textbook with My Throbbing Penis

(see course title)

Intro to Shiv Making

Life is full of surprises and you never know when you might have to create an improvised weapon that will protect your cigarette stash or save your life. Whether a suburban WASP or an inner city BLACK, this course will provide you with the resource identification, time management, and craftsmanship necessary to create and wield a sharpened toothbrush, bedspring, or mop handle. Fulfills Physical Education requirement. Protective eyewear is recommended but not mandatory.

Important

Very. 3 credits.

Pizza Party: The How and Who's

The days of renting a VHS tape and expecting our young people to lounge around with one cheese, one pepperoni, and one everything pizza (for Mom and Dad) are behind us. It's time to welcome cheese, melted on sauce, smeared upon baked bread to the internet age. Today's children want options. What does that mean and how can you keep 13 tweens from committing a mass suicide in your downstairs playroom? Two words: A Pizza Party.

The Snacks of the Byzantine Empire

Long before Fun-Yuns and Gushers dominated the modern market, the wise and industrious people of Constantinople were praised for their bite-sized edibles. From the unchewable "Byzy bites" to the rash-inducing "Macedonian Nuts", no other empire during the Middle Age created such splendid confections. This class will not only introduce students to the production and distribution of these ancient treats but will also examine the roles of the fat asses who created these timeless recipes.

The Art of Walking

Take a breath. Now hold. Now exhale. Feet. Welcome to The Art of Walking. Please join me, your instructor, Felice Montay as I guide you, step-by-step, into the world of Walking. Our journey will begin the moment you enter the classroom. I will personally take off your shoes and introduce your toes and your heels and your perfectly imperfect foot wrinkles to the stage we call…Earth. Walking is the first dance we all learn and I think that is important. Don't you?

The Rhetoric of Hard-Core Pornography

A course about words and meaning in the age of readily accessible ass play. Students must be able to handle pornographic language, visuals and live demonstrations without arousal. Seriously, keep your cum guns and beef holes dry. 3 credits.

Made in the USA
Middletown, DE
04 February 2023